33
MEZ

GIANT VEHICLES
An Imagination Library Series

GIANT TRACTORS

Jim Mezzanotte

GARETH**STEVENS**
GS
PUBLISHING
A Member of the WRC Media Family of Companies

Please visit our web site at: www.garethstevens.com
For a free color catalog describing Gareth Stevens Publishing's list of high-quality books and multimedia programs, call 1-800-542-2595 (USA) or 1-800-387-3178 (Canada). Gareth Stevens Publishing's fax: (414) 332-3567.

Library of Congress Cataloging-in-Publication Data

Mezzanotte, Jim.
    Giant tractors / by Jim Mezzanotte.
        p. cm. — (Giant vehicles)
    Includes bibliographical references and index.
    ISBN 0-8368-4915-9 (lib. bdg.)
    ISBN 0-8368-4922-1 (softcover)
    1. Tractors—Juvenile literature. I. Title.
    TL233.15.M49   2005
    629.225'2—dc22   2005045156

First published in 2006 by
Gareth Stevens Publishing
A Member of the WRC Media Family of Companies
330 West Olive Street, Suite 100
Milwaukee, WI 53212 USA

Editorial direction: Mark J. Sachner
Editor: JoAnn Early Macken
Art direction: Tammy West
Cover design and page layout: Kami M. Koenig
Photo editor: Diane Laska-Swanke
Picture researcher: Martin Levick

Photo credits: Cover, pp. 5, 7, 9, 11, 15, 17, 19, 21 Reproduced with permission by CNH America LLC; p. 13 © Eric Orlemann

Printed in the United States of America

1 2 3 4 5 6 7 8 9 09 08 07 06 05

COVER: Giant tractors are tough, powerful machines. On big farms, they do all kinds of jobs.

Table of Contents

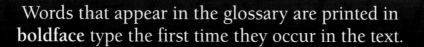

Words that appear in the glossary are printed in **boldface** type the first time they occur in the text.

Farmer's Helper

Giant tractors pull things. They are mostly used on big farms. They pull all kinds of machines. The machines do many jobs. They **plow** the earth. They plant **crops**. Giant tractors work fast so farmers can finish big jobs quickly.

A giant tractor needs good **traction** for pulling. Most giant tractors use many huge tires. One tractor may have twelve tires! The tractors have powerful engines, too.

On a large farm, there is a lot to do. Giant tractors are always working. They even work at night. They have to be tough and reliable.

This giant tractor is pulling scrapers. They scrape the ground to move large amounts of dirt. The tractor needs a lot of pulling power for this job.

Bigger and Better

The first tractors were built in the 1800s. Most did not work well on farms. They were heavy and slow. Their metal wheels crushed the soil. By the 1930s, tractors were much better. They had strong, reliable engines. They traveled quickly on big rubber tires. The tires had good traction. They did not crush the ground.

Tractors changed farming. With tractors, more work could be done by fewer people.

By the 1960s, many farms were huge. Large farms needed large tractors. The tractors kept growing. Engine power grew, too. Many farmers began using giant tractors.

The Steiger company made this Panther model in the 1970s. By then, many farmers were using giant tractors. They could do more work than smaller tractors.

Big Wheels

On a giant tractor, each wheel has two or three tires. With more tires, each tire holds less weight. If a tire held more weight, it would press down hard on the dirt. Plants would not grow well in this dirt.

Most giant tractors have four-wheel drive. Their engines turn all four wheels. All those tires grip the earth. The tractors have great pulling power.

Giant tractors bend in the middle! The front and back halves are on a big hinge. The front wheels do not steer left or right. When the farmer steers, the whole front turns.

On this tractor, power goes to eight big wheels. The tires have thick ridges for gripping the ground. When the farmer steers, the whole front turns right or left.

Traveling on Tracks

A giant tractor may have no tires at all. Instead, it may have **tracks**. The tracks are rubber belts. The belts circle around a row of wheels. The wide tracks spread out the tractor's weight. A lot of rubber grips the earth. The tractors have good traction. They are not as wide as tractors with many tires.

Some tractors have two long tracks. There is one track on each side. To turn, the farmer makes one track spin faster. Other tractors have four smaller tracks. There is one at each corner where the wheel would be. These tractors bend in the middle like tractors with wheels.

This Steiger tractor has four tracks. In each track, the wheel on top turns the rubber belt. The tractor bends in the middle. You can see where it bends.

Tractor Power

Tractors use **diesel** engines. These engines are similar to car engines. But they use diesel **fuel**, not gasoline. They are much larger than car engines. They produce a lot more **horsepower**. Tractor engines use **turbochargers** for more power.

Farm machines have moving parts. A tractor makes these parts move. The tractor has a tube in back. The engine spins the tube. This tube connects to a farm machine. It makes parts in the machine move. A tractor engine also creates **hydraulic** power. The engine pumps oil. The force of this oil can move the parts in farm machines, too.

The John Deere company made this giant tractor. It has a powerful engine for turning its large wheels. It will not get stuck—not even in this muddy field!

Inside the Cab

A giant tractor has a comfortable cab. The cab makes the farmer's job easier. The windows are large for seeing all around. The cab has heat and air-conditioning. The seat rides on a cushion of air. The cab even has a CD player!

The cab has a steering wheel like a car. It has many switches and levers. Some control the tractor. Others control the farm machines. When you drive a tractor, you have a lot to do! Today, farmers use computers to help them do their jobs. The cab has a computer screen. It even has a place for a farmer's **laptop**!

This cab makes working easier. It has big windows all around. It has levers at your fingertips. In heat or cold, it keeps you comfortable.

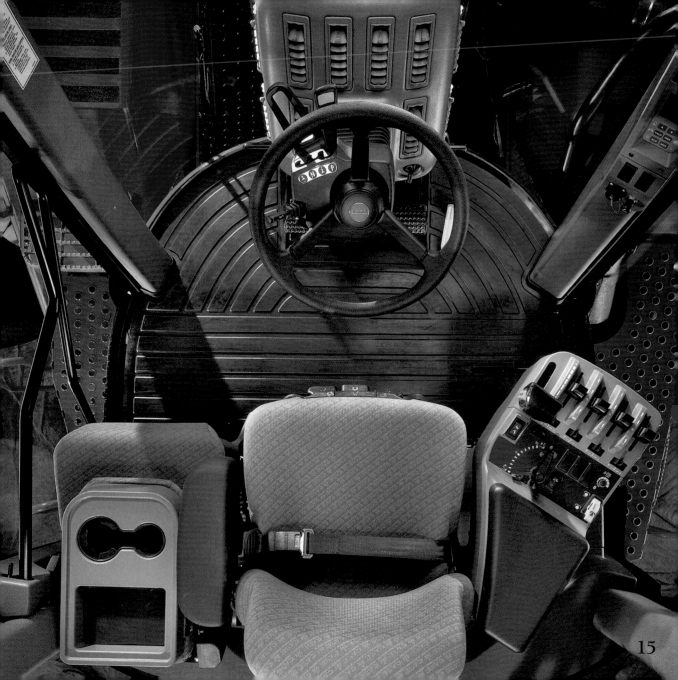

How Big Is Big?

Giant tractors are smaller than other huge machines. But they are still big! They are twice as tall as an adult. To reach the cab, you have to climb a ladder. Some wheels are taller than many adults.

Tractors are heavy. They are made of thick steel. They can weigh over 15 tons — ten times more than some cars. The tractors hold a lot of fuel. Most cars hold less than 20 gallons (75 liters) of fuel. A tractor may hold 270 gallons (1,000 l) of fuel!

Giant tractors work quickly. A giant tractor could plow ten football fields in one hour!

In a giant tractor, you sit high in the air. You climb steps to reach the cab. This tractor has a lot of work to do. It will get the work done quickly!

Tractor Makers

Over the years, many companies built giant tractors. One company was Steiger. Two brothers started this company in the 1950s. They were farmers. They wanted a better tractor, so they built their own. It had four-wheel drive. Soon, many farmers used Steiger tractors. "Big Bud" was another giant tractor. It had twice the power of other big tractors.

Today, Steiger tractors are still made. A company called Case IH makes them. The John Deere Company also makes giant tractors. It has made farm equipment for more than one hundred years. The Buhler Company makes giant tractors, too.

These men work at Case New Holland. They are finishing some new tractors. Case New Holland makes many farm machines, including Steiger tractors.

Tractors at Work

Giant tractors pull many kinds of machines. Plowing machines dig into the ground and turn it over so it is ready for planting. Cultivators loosen dirt so plants grow better. Drills shoot seeds into the ground. Other machines spray **fertilizer**.

It takes skill to drive a giant tractor. You have to control the tractor and the farming machine. The many tires have to roll between the rows of plants. You do not want to crush those plants! At night, you may have to keep working. The tractor has powerful lights. On a farm, there is always more work to do!

This giant tractor is pulling a big load of grain. On a farm, a tractor pulls many different machines. It keeps working, day after day!

More to Read and View

Books

Farm Machines. Let's See Library (series). Jennifer Blizin Gillis (Compass Point Books)

Farm Tractors. Mighty Movers (series). Sarah Tieck (Buddy Books)

Farm Tractors. Pull Ahead Transportation (series). Kristin C. Nelson (Lerner Publishing)

The Rusty, Trusty Tractor. Joy Cowley (Boyds Mills Press)

Tractors. Machines at Work (series). Caroline Bingham (DK Publishing)

The Usborne Book of Tractors. Young Machines (series). Caroline Young (E.D.C. Publishing)

Videos

All About John Deere for Kids (Consumervision)

Big Equipment: Farm Machinery (United American Video)

Farming for Kids (Blackboard Entertainment)

There Goes a Tractor Real Wheels (series) (A Vision)

Web Sites

Web sites change frequently, but we believe the following web sites are going to last. You can also use good search engines, such as **Yahooligans!** (www.yahooligans.com) or **Google** (www.google.com) to find more information about giant vehicles. Some keywords that will help you are *Big Bud, Buhler, Case IH, diesel engines, farm machinery, John Deere, Steiger,* and *tractors.*

science.howstuffworks.com/
 hydraulic.htm
Visit this web site to learn more about how hydraulic machines work.

www.bigtractorpower.com/
This web site has a history of four-wheel drive tractors. The site also has many pictures of different giant tractors.

www.buhler.com/sitefiles/product/
 tractor/versatile/versatile.htm
At this web site, you can learn all about Buhler four-wheel drive tractors. The site has information and many pictures. Click "pictures" to see them.

www.caseih.com/products/series.aspx
 ?lineid=2&seriesid=14&navid=
 105&RL=ENNA
This web page is from the Case IH web site. Visit it to learn all about the newest Steiger tractors.

auto.howstuffworks.com/diesel1.htm
This web site shows how a diesel engine works.

www.deere.com/en_US/Product
 Catalog/FR/category/FR_
 tractors.html
Visit this site to learn about John Deere giant tractors. You can also learn about the different machines the tractors pull.

www.historylink101.com/lessons/
 farm-city/modern_farm_ tractors.htm
This site has pictures of several tractors, including giant tractors. It also has pictures of machines the tractors pull.

www.meissners.com/pages/bigbud.
 html
At this site, learn all about Big Bud tractors. The site has pictures, too.

Glossary

You can find these words on the pages listed. Reading a word in a sentence helps you to understand it even better.

crops (KRAHPS): the plants that a farmer grows. 4

diesel (DEE-zull): the name for a kind of engine and the special fuel it uses. Most diesel engines are very reliable. They often use less fuel than gas engines. 12

fertilizer (FUR-tuh-lye-zur): something put into soil to make plants grow better. 20

fuel (FYULE): something that burns to provide energy. 12, 16

horsepower (HORS-pow-ur): the amount of power an engine makes, based on how much work one horse can do. 12

hydraulic (hi-DRAW-lick): having to do with using water or another liquid to move something. 12

laptop (LAP-top): a computer small enough to fit on your lap. 14

plow (PLOW): dig into and turn over ground to get it ready for planting crops. 4, 16, 20

tracks (TRAX): belts that circle around a row of wheels to move a machine. One wheel in each belt makes it turn. Some tracks are metal plates linked together. Other tracks are loops made of rubber. 10

traction (TRAK-shun): the grip that something has on a surface. To pull things, a tractor's tires or tracks need a good grip on the ground. 4, 6, 10

turbocharger (TUR-boe-char-jur): a device that forces more air into an engine, giving it more power. 12

Index